Original title:
A Chill in the Air

Author: Aron Pilviste
ISBN HARDBACK: 978-9916-79-483-8
ISBN PAPERBACK: 978-9916-79-484-5
ISBN EBOOK: 978-9916-79-485-2

Night's Cloak and Day's Respite

In shadows deep, the stars ignite,
A canvas draped in velvet night.
Whispers soft, the moonlight spills,
Embracing dreams on quiet hills.

The sun prepares to take its flight,
As dawn unfurls in hues of light.
With every glow, a promise made,
In day's embrace, the night will fade.

The Veil Between Seasons

In winter's chill, the silence grows,
A white expanse where soft wind blows.
Yet spring awakens, buds unfurl,
Life dances forth, a joyous whirl.

The leaves do change, a golden hue,
As summer's warmth brings skies so blue.
Each gentle shift, a time to greet,
The cycle turns, a rhythmic beat.

Gentle Caress of Bitter Winds

The north winds howl like restless tides,
They twist and turn, where secret hides.
Yet with their chill comes whispered song,
A bittersweet embrace so strong.

Through barren trees, their fingers crawl,
A haunted call, a nature's thrall.
But in the frost, there's beauty found,
As hearts beat loud on icy ground.

Mourning the Blossoms

Upon the boughs where petals fell,
A fragrant past, a wistful spell.
In hues of pink, their beauty shone,
Yet time moves on, their essence gone.

The breeze now carries tales of old,
Of summer days and warmth untold.
As silence falls where blooms once thrived,
In memory's clasp, their spirit's alive.

Whispers of the Fading Sun

The golden rays draw close,
As shadows begin to spin.
Silent echoes linger slow,
In the day's soft, warm skin.

With every breath of twilight,
The sky blushes deep in grace.
Nature sings her sweet goodbyes,
In this fading, sacred space.

Colors dance on gentle waves,
While horizons softly sigh.
Whispers of a day well spent,
Underneath the twilight sky.

The last light kisses the earth,
As stars prepare to shine bright.
Moments wrapped in sweet repose,
Embrace the coming night.

Serpents of Fog on the Lake

Misty tendrils weave and twist,
Caressing shores with their breath.
A dance of secrets in the night,
Hiding whispers, tales of death.

The moonlight glimmers on the waves,
As shadows slip beneath the deep.
Serpents curl through the silence,
Guarding dreams that we must keep.

Each ripple tells a story lost,
In the depths where echoes trace.
The fog entwines like ancient ghosts,
In this haunting, whispered space.

Nature's breath draws heavy still,
As the water holds its peace.
Serpents fade into the shadows,
In a night that won't release.

A Soft Yet Stinging Embrace

The wind whispers through the trees,
A gentle touch, yet sharp and cold.
It wraps around like tender hands,
A moment sweet, yet fierce and bold.

With every rustle, every sigh,
The heart learns both the joy and pain.
Emotions dance like autumn leaves,
Fleeting, yet they leave a stain.

This embrace, a braided thread,
Of love entwined with bitter doubt.
A softness veils the sharper edge,
As weary souls begin to shout.

In the quiet, feelings surge,
A paradox that feels so real.
A memory, both sweet and sharp,
In every breath, a hidden zeal.

The Album of the Fallen Leaves

Each leaf a page, turned with care,
Swirling down in autumn's breath.
Colors of the past unfold,
In gilded warmth, they dance with death.

A crisp scent fills the golden air,
Stories whispered through the boughs.
Memories, like leaves, reside,
Reflecting time in solemn vows.

Through amber skies and twilight hues,
Nature's brush paints on the grove.
An album filled with laughter's tears,
As seasons weave the tales we love.

In every rustle, silence speaks,
The beauty lies in what's let go.
Fallen leaves, a testament,
To life's rich tale of ebb and flow.

Solitude Wrapped in Mist

In the dawn's soft embrace, we hide,
Whispers of dreams, where shadows glide.
Veils of fog dance in muted light,
Silence sings, as day meets night.

Footsteps vanish, lost in the haze,
The world fades, in this gentle maze.
Nature's breath, so calm and deep,
In this solitude, my heart can weep.

Echoes linger in the stillness round,
Every heartbeat like a call profound.
The mist cradles thoughts yet to bloom,
Wrapped in a tapestry that whispers gloom.

Moments stretch, like shadows at play,
Time stands still as night meets day.
In solitude, the soul takes flight,
Finding peace in the cloak of night.

Here, in the embrace of the cool, wet air,
Emotions unfurl, stripped down and bare.
Wrapped in mist, I find my space,
A sanctuary, a sacred place.

Sable Skies and Dewy Grass

Underneath the sable skies,
Dreams awaken, like soft sighs.
Dewy grass beneath my feet,
Nature's kiss, so cool, so sweet.

Stars peek through the velvet cloak,
Whispers shared, unspoken hopes.
The night's embrace, a lullaby,
As shadows dance and time drifts by.

Moments glisten in the dark,
Each heartbeat like a glowing spark.
A universe in every drop,
In this garden, we'll never stop.

Whispers roam on the midnight breeze,
A soft rhythm that puts us at ease.
With every breath, a tale unfolds,
As the night's embrace gently holds.

In the quiet, we are free,
Sable skies, our symphony.
With dew-kissed dreams and hearts so bold,
We weave our stories, bright as gold.

The Quietude of an Approaching Storm

Air thickens with whispers low,
Clouds gather, a solemn show.
The horizon darkens with intent,
A quietude that feels well-meant.

Trees shiver in a breathless pause,
Nature holds with gentle jaws.
Lightning's kiss waits in the wings,
Ready to unleash its fierce offerings.

Time stretches, a taut, drawn line,
Each heartbeat syncs, a warning sign.
In this stillness, tension thrives,
As anticipation hums, alive.

Moments last, yet swiftly fade,
In the heart, a tempest laid.
The quietude wraps around tight,
Breeding chaos; a storm ignites.

In the clash of thunder's roar,
The world shifts, forevermore.
In the lull, we find our place,
Embracing the storm with fierce grace.

Memories of Flame Doused in Blue

Flickers fade in the twilight's grip,
Embers dance on a forgotten trip.
Memories linger in soft refrain,
A tapestry woven with joy and pain.

Blue hues wash over silent nights,
As whispers weave through lost delights.
Each flame a story, now turned to ash,
In the depths where shadows clash.

Moments captured in a breath,
A life lived fully, beyond death.
The warmth of flames fades to hue,
Yet in reflections, we find what's true.

In the quiet, echoes resound,
Past flames flickering, lost yet found.
With every change, the heart learns anew,
Life's ember glows, doused in blue.

Memories swirl, a gentle tide,
As the heart keeps love inside.
Though flames may wane, their spirits soar,
In the silence, they dance once more.

When Trees Stand Still

When trees stand still, their shadows play,
In whispers soft, they greet the day.
Leaves hold their breath, a secret shared,
Roots embrace the earth, gently cared.

Branches dream of skies so wide,
In silent vows, they stand with pride.
The sun dips low, the colors blend,
In twilight's hush, the moments bend.

Soft winds sigh through boughs so green,
Nature's canvas, calm and serene.
A world unfolds beneath the stars,
As night descends, we count the scars.

Each tree a story, history unfolds,
In stillness found, the nature holds.
A watchful eye on time's soft flow,
In every shade, the seasons grow.

So when trees stand still, take a while,
Stop for a moment, breathe, and smile.
For in their presence, peace resides,
In nature's heart, the truth abides.

In the Wake of a Winter's Tale

In the wake of winter's tale so bold,
Blankets of white, a world now cold.
Snowflakes dance, in the quiet air,
Whispers of warmth, a dream to share.

Frosty breath paints the window panes,
Echoes of laughter, lingering strains.
Footprints soft on a carpet bright,
Memories etched in the crisp night.

Trees stand bare, their branches stark,
Silent witnesses in the dark.
Under the stars, a hush prevails,
Nature's lullabies, woven trails.

The air is sharp, but hearts are warm,
Against the chill, we weather the storm.
In cozy nooks, we cozy abide,
With tales of wonder woven inside.

So let the winter tale unfold,
With every glance, new stories told.
In the wake of snow, we find our way,
Through whispered dreams of a brighter day.

The Tension of a Late Frost

The tension of a late frost hangs,
In morning's glow, a silence clangs.
Buds hold tight with a fragile plea,
Awaiting spring's warm symphony.

Icy fingers touch the ground,
Where life lurks close, but still unbound.
Nature holds its breath in dread,
As sunlight creeps, fears are fed.

Dewdrops glisten on the leaves,
In the quiet, the heart believes.
A chill remains as shadows creep,
In whispered dreams, the world does weep.

But hope is forged in winter's chill,
With every strand of light, a thrill.
For in the dawn, the warmth will call,
Life's resilience will conquer all.

So let the late frost weave its tale,
A dance of seasons, a fragile frail.
In every moment, tension sings,
Waiting for the joy that springtime brings.

Hushed Conversations of the Night

Hushed conversations of the night,
In shadows deep, the stars ignite.
Whispers float on a gentle breeze,
Carried softly through the trees.

Moonlight dances on the skin,
With every breath, the stories spin.
Animals stir in secret places,
In nature's arms, they find their spaces.

Crickets chirp a soothing song,
As time slips past where we belong.
The velvet sky wraps us in grace,
As dreams unfold in this sacred space.

Night unfolds like a velvet page,
In the silence, we turn the stage.
The world outside takes a deep breath,
In the calm of night, we confront death.

Hushed conversations, stars convene,
In the stillness, a world unseen.
With every heartbeat, secrets lie,
In the gentle whisper of the sky.

Winter's Whisper

The snow falls soft, a gentle kiss,
Whispers of cold, a fleeting bliss.
Bare trees stand proud, in silence they keep,
Secrets of winter, as dreams drift to sleep.

Icicles hang like crystal tears,
Time slows down, quieting fears.
Footprints linger in the powdery white,
Marking the path of a long, cold night.

The moon aglow, a guardian bright,
Guides the lost through the tranquil night.
Stars blink softly, a distant choir,
Echoing warmth in the chill of desire.

Beneath thick blankets, hearts begin to yearn,
For fireside stories, where embers burn.
Hot cocoa calling, wrapped in the glow,
Winter's embrace, where warmth starts to flow.

As dawn awakens with hues of gold,
Winter whispers tales anew, retold.
Nature's breath, a frosty sigh,
In this quiet season, we learn to fly.

Frosted Breath

Morning breaks with a frosted breath,
Nature's canvas, declaring death.
Branches glisten, like diamonds bound,
Whispers of silence, a soft, sweet sound.

Fields of white blanket the sleeping earth,
Each flake a story, each drift, a birth.
A chill sends shivers down spines anew,
Yet warmth lingers, in hearts it grew.

Children bundled, with laughter and cheer,
Chasing the snowflakes that dance, so near.
Snowmen rise with their carrot noses,
Greeting the day, as winter dozes.

As twilight falls, the colors fade,
Stars peek down, through the winking shade.
Air crisp and clear, dreams take their flight,
In the stillness, the world feels right.

Frosted breath lingers beyond the trees,
Whispers of magic carried by the breeze.
Wrapped in layers, snug and tight,
The beauty of winter, a glorious sight.

Echoes of Autumn's Embrace

Leaves turn gold, a brilliant dance,
Whimsical whispers, a fleeting chance.
Crisp air carries the scent of change,
A tapestry woven, colors so strange.

Pumpkins glow under the harvest moon,
Fields of plenty, a bountiful tune.
Wind sings softly through branches bare,
Echoes of life linger everywhere.

Sweaters pulled tight as shadows grow,
Fires crackle, casting a warm glow.
Stories unfold by the evening light,
Wrapped in warmth, everything feels right.

In the fading sun, whispers collide,
Time moving slow, as moments abide.
Autumn's embrace, a bittersweet kiss,
Nature's farewell, a poignant bliss.

As twilight deepens, the chill sets in,
Yet memories linger, where joy begins.
With every rustle, every soft sigh,
Echoes of autumn, we cherish and fly.

The Silent Shiver

A breath of wind sends a silent shiver,
Through fields yet sleeping, where shadows quiver.
Frosty mists rise with the break of dawn,
Veiling the world that the night has drawn.

Branches entwined in a lace of ice,
Nature whispers secrets, calm and precise.
Birds have taken their quiet flight,
Leaving behind echoes of soft delight.

The lake lies still, a mirror of gray,
Reflecting the solemnness of the day.
Ripples dance lightly, as time ticks slow,
A silent serenade in the winter's glow.

With each step forward, the crunching sound,
Marks the arrival of light all around.
Yet shadows linger, from a world once bright,
In the grip of the shiver, we seek the light.

As night descends, the stars appear,
Breaking the silence, they twinkle near.
In the stillness, we find a way,
To embrace the shiver that leads to day.

The Language of the Falling Leaves

Whispers in the rustling trees,
Golden hues dance with the breeze.
Nature's secrets shared in flight,
Autumn speaks in colors bright.

Crisp sounds echo on the ground,
Stories in each leaf are found.
Tales of life, love, and decay,
In their fall, they softly sway.

Crimson, amber, brown, and gold,
Each one has a story told.
Gentle sighs as they descend,
Nature's words that never end.

Gather them in silent prayer,
Memories drift through the air.
Listen close, their voices weave,
The language of the falling leaves.

In the twilight's fading glow,
Where the chilly rivers flow.
Nature's choir starts to sing,
In the crispness of the spring.

Frosted Footsteps on Forgotten Trails

A blanket white on paths of old,
Stories in the frost unfold.
Footsteps left in morning dew,
Whispers of the lost and true.

Each step crackles, crisp and clear,
Echoes of those once held dear.
Silent tales in ice etched deep,
Secrets that the mountains keep.

Through the woods, the shadows play,
Frosted whispers guide the way.
Memory's breath in fleeting chill,
The stillness warms the heart, until.

Branches bow with laden grace,
Nature's beauty finds its place.
Upon the trails where few have tread,
Dreams of many left unsaid.

With each breath, the cold invites,
To find solace in the nights.
Wander on, where few prevail,
In frosted footsteps on the trail.

Glacial Whispers of Dusk

As daylight dims into the night,
Glacial whispers soften light.
The world adorned in silver lace,
As shadows deepen, time slows pace.

Icebergs float in twilight's arms,
Serenading with their charms.
The sky blushes in muted hues,
Nature's canvas, deep and true.

Waves of silence brush the shore,
Each whisper hints at ancient lore.
Stars begin their nightly waltz,
In the quiet, time halts.

Breath of winter chills the air,
Nights bring forth a gentle care.
Underneath the icy veil,
Glacial whispers tell the tale.

In this moment, still and vast,
Hold the echoes of the past.
As dusk entwines with night's embrace,
Find the beauty in this space.

Where Darkness Meets the Icy Dawn

In the hush of fading night,
Stars retreat from morning light.
Chill of shadows lingers near,
As dawn approaches, bright and clear.

Whispers wrap the world so tight,
Nightfall yields to morning's might.
The earth awakens, soft and slow,
Painting skies with vibrant glow.

Frosted grass with glimmers shines,
A canvas rich with silver lines.
Breath of warmth begins to rise,
In this dance where darkness dies.

Light spills forth like molten gold,
Stories of new days unfold.
Each moment brightens, fears are gone,
Where darkness meets the icy dawn.

Embrace the day, let spirits soar,
With every sunrise, seek for more.
In harmony, the world reborn,
At the edge of light, forlorn.

November's Lament

Leaves fall gently, whispers soft,
The chill creeps in, feelings loft.
Days grow short, shadows blend,
A quiet sorrow, none to mend.

Memories linger, bittersweet,
Echoes of laughter, now discreet.
Fires flicker with fading light,
Cold embraces the quiet night.

Ghosts of summer, lost to time,
Crisp air carries a weary rhyme.
Nature weeps in muted tones,
As winter calls the earth to moans.

Branches bare, the world stands still,
Dreams dissolve like morning's thrill.
November sighs, a heavy weight,
Awaiting hope that winter's fate.

In this pause, a chance to yearn,
For brighter days, for life to learn.
In solemn grace, we turn within,
Embracing loss, yet seeking kin.

The Hour When Time Stands Still

In twilight's glow, the world does cease,
A moment's breath, a whispered peace.
Echo soft, like distant chimes,
The hour sings in muted rhymes.

Stars unveil in velvet skies,
Each glimmer holds forgotten sighs.
In stillness, shadows twist and sway,
As thoughts drift in a dreamlike play.

The clock's hands pause, no race to run,
All is calm when day is done.
In heartbeat's echo, silence swells,
A tranquil spell, no words can tell.

Time stretches thin, like fading light,
Lost in reverie, not shy of night.
All around, the air is hushed,
In this hour of calm, we trust.

In dreams we weave, we find our way,
As echoes of night give rise to day.
Time may flee, yet love remains,
In the stillness, we break chains.

Frostbitten Reminiscence

Frost clings gently to the pane,
A world of crystal, sharp and plain.
Memories shimmer, cold and bright,
Wrapped in whispers of the night.

Voices fade within the mist,
Friends and laughter, none to twist.
In frozen frames, our hearts encase,
The warmth of love we long to trace.

Winter's breath, a chilling song,
Recalling where we once belonged.
Through icy paths our thoughts will roam,
Yet in our hearts, we find a home.

A touch of warmth in bitter air,
Brings forth the laughter, light and rare.
Frostbits fall, like tears we shed,
In every flake, our stories spread.

Time moves on, yet here we stay,
Bound by memories, come what may.
Through winters cold, we'll find the sun,
In reminiscence, we are one.

A Dance of the Forgotten Winds

Silent breezes through the trees,
Whisper tales of ancient seas.
Dancing softly, shadows play,
In twilight's grip, they drift away.

Leaves may tremble, spirits spin,
Voices of the past begin.
In the hush, the echoes glide,
Forgotten dreams that still abide.

Winds of change, so crisp and clear,
Summon whispers, draw them near.
Through empty fields and open skies,
A haunting melody replies.

Ghostly dances, fleeting grace,
In every sigh, a warm embrace.
A net of time, woven tight,
Twists and turns in fading light.

As dusk unfolds, the winds take flight,
Carrying secrets into night.
In their journey, hopes are cast,
A dance that binds our futures past.

The Edge of Remembrance

In whispers soft, the past does call,
Echoes linger, shadows fall.
Memories dance like fading light,
Recollections in the night.

Through alleyways where silence dwells,
Stories trapped in ancient shells.
Fleeting moments, bittersweet,
Where joy and sorrow ever meet.

Old photographs in frames so worn,
Frayed edges tell of love reborn.
Haunting dreams in twilight fade,
A tapestry of memories made.

Beneath the stars, a heart does yearn,
For whispered secrets, lessons learned.
In every heartbeat, time we trace,
The edge of remembrance, our sacred place.

As seasons change and years go by,
We hold the past with a gentle sigh.
For in our hearts, it ever thrives,
The edge of remembrance, where love survives.

In the Grip of Winter's Hold

Chill winds whisper through the trees,
Blanketing earth with frozen ease.
Crisp air bites at fingertips,
Winter's breath on frosted lips.

Silent nights with stars aglow,
Nature sleeps beneath the snow.
Footprints trace a path once bold,
Now lost in winter's icy hold.

Branches bare, a stark display,
Of life in pause, in shades of gray.
Yet in this stillness, hope remains,
A promise whispered through the pains.

In cozy nooks, we gather tight,
By the fire's warm, inviting light.
Stories shared, laughter unfolds,
In the grip of winter's hold.

The world transforms to crystal dreams,
Flowing rivers now frozen streams.
In every flake, a tale is spun,
Winter's reign is never done.

Possibilities in the Glistening Frost

Morning breaks in radiant hues,
A world reborn with sparkly views.
Each blade of grass dons icy lace,
A shimmering coat, nature's embrace.

In the quiet, dreams take flight,
Possibilities dance in soft daylight.
With every breath, fresh chances bloom,
Life awakens from winter's gloom.

Wander paths where vision shines,
In wonderland, fate intertwines.
With open hearts, we seek to find,
The magic woven through mankind.

Frosty whispers call us near,
Every moment, bright and clear.
In each reflection, stories tossed,
In the glistening frost, what's gained, not lost.

Held in silence, beauty's grace,
Possibilities, a timeless chase.
In nature's arms, we dare to dream,
In every sparkle, hope's soft gleam.

Beneath the Silvered Canopy

In twilight's hush, the world transforms,
Beneath the silvered canopy, life warms.
Leaves shimmer in the evening light,
A dance of shadows takes to flight.

Silent whispers fill the air,
Nature's secrets everywhere.
Moonlit paths we wander wide,
Underneath the stars, our guide.

In tranquil moments, hearts unite,
Lost in dreams that feel so right.
With every step, the night unveils,
The beauty in a thousand tales.

Raindrops kissed by starlit beams,
In the quiet, flow our dreams.
Beneath the silvered leaves we sway,
In the symphony of night and day.

Each breath a promise, each glance a spark,
The wonders found in shadows dark.
Beneath the canopy, we feel alive,
In every moment, together we thrive.

Fragile Beauty of Fading Light

As daylight wanes, hues intertwine,
Soft whispers dance, a fleeting sign.
Shadows stretch, embrace the night,
Fragile beauty in fading light.

Petals droop, their colors fade,
In twilight's grasp, memories laid.
Time's gentle touch, a tender feel,
Moments cherished, forever real.

The stars awaken, bold and bright,
While echoes linger, soft as flight.
Each fleeting glance, a tender call,
What once was vibrant, now gently falls.

Yet in this dusk, a promise glows,
A cycle renewed, as nature knows.
From decay springs forth new delight,
In fragile beauty of fading light.

The Echoes of Distant Wings

Across the sky, a shadowed grace,
Whispers travel, in boundless space.
Birds on the wing, through air they soar,
The echoes call, forevermore.

In twilight's hush, their songs resound,
Melodies woven, a tapestry profound.
Each flutter tells a tale of sky,
Of freedom's strive, of how to fly.

Beneath the stars, their paths ignite,
In silent flight, they claim the night.
From mountain tops to oceans deep,
The echoes of wings in dreams we keep.

A gentle breeze, a lover's sigh,
Carrying hopes as they drift by.
In nature's choir, we find our wings,
The echoes soften, as the heart sings.

Echoing Footfalls in the Frost

Crunching snow beneath, a fleeting sound,
Footfalls echoing all around.
In winter's grasp, a world stands still,
Each step a whisper, a heart to fill.

Branches bare, with diamonds bright,
Glistening softly in pale moonlight.
The air is sharp, yet dreams take flight,
Echoing footfalls in the frost tonight.

Silence reigns, yet stories speak,
Of journeys made, of paths we seek.
Each print a mark of where we've been,
In the wake of frost, life's cinnamon spin.

As shadows extend and night draws near,
The world seems quiet, yet ever near.
With every tread, memories are tossed,
Echoing footfalls, no moment lost.

The Lingering Breath of a Spent Warmth

Fires once bright, now dying embers,
In whispered tones, the heart remembers.
In every flicker, a story told,
The lingering breath of warmth so bold.

Soft glowing hues, now dimmed to grey,
Yet within the ashes, warmth will stay.
Close your eyes, feel the embrace,
Of memories wrapped in time's soft lace.

The chill of dusk begins to creep,
Yet echoes of laughter, sweet and deep.
In shadows cast, love's glow remains,
The lingering breath of warmth sustains.

With every moment that slips away,
We hold those treasures, come what may.
In quiet whispers, our hearts will strive,
For warmth is not lost, but kept alive.

Finality in the Promised Silence

In twilight's hush, shadows dance,
Whispers fade, lost in the trance.
Embracing stillness, dreams take flight,
Finality weaves through the night.

Crickets sing their sweet refrain,
Echoes linger, pulse the pain.
A heart once bold, now draped in gloom,
Silence reigns, an endless tomb.

Stars unveil their distant glow,
Guiding souls to paths we know.
Beneath the vast, embracing sky,
We find the strength to say goodbye.

Time slips softly, grain by grain,
Memories wrapped in mist and rain.
Eternity whispers in our ears,
Finality dissolves our fears.

In promised silence, peace descends,
A journey starts, a journey mends.
With every breath, we learn, we grow,
In quiet corners, love's seeds sow.

Frosty Whispers Among the Pines

Beneath the trees, the frost does cling,
Nature's breath, a gentle sting.
Whispers echo in the cold,
Secrets of the forest told.

Pines stand tall, a silent guard,
Every branch, a tranquil bard.
In the crisp, the shadows play,
Frosty whispers, night and day.

Snowflakes dance through beams of light,
Crafting magic, pure and bright.
Footsteps crunch on frozen ground,
In the quiet, peace is found.

Wind brings tales from distant lands,
Carried softly through snowy strands.
In the stillness, hearts combine,
Sharing warmth, as stars align.

Among the pines, the world feels new,
Nature's canvas, painted blue.
Frosty whispers, a bond divine,
In each moment, the stars align.

The Edge of Day Meets the Frigid Night

At dusk the sky begins to breathe,
Where daylight, slow, begins to leave.
Colors clash in a cosmic fight,
The edge of day greets frigid night.

Shadows stretch long, embracing dusk,
Nature's heart begins to husk.
With every hue, a story's spun,
As warmth succumbs to night's cold run.

Stars awaken, shy and bright,
Winking softly, stealing light.
The moon ascends, a silver queen,
Over fields of twilight green.

In the silence, whispers call,
Echoes of dusk begin to fall.
Every breath, a fleeting glance,
The night invites a daring dance.

As night unfolds, dreams take flight,
At the edge of day, it's pure delight.
In the cool embrace of night's cocoon,
We find our solace beneath the moon.

Fragile Moments Before the Thaw

The world holds its breath, then sighs,
As sunlight dances on snow's white guise.
Underneath, the earth stirs and waits,
Whispers of spring at the garden gates.

A fragile warmth caresses the chill,
Promises of blooms begin to spill.
Buds peek cautiously from the ground,
In these soft moments, hope is found.

Yesterday's frost begins to fade,
Dreams of green, the sun has laid.
Nature's brush strokes with gentle care,
Painting the world, beyond compare.

Each glimmering drop, a glistening tear,
Mirrors of joy, and fleeting fear.
For with each thaw, life's journey flows,
An endless cycle, as nature knows.

So linger a while in the twilight glow,
Embrace the change, let the heart show.
For in the thaw, all things revive,
In fragile moments, we truly thrive.

Shadows Amidst the Twinkling Ice

Beneath the moon, the shadows play,
Twinkling ice, where dreams delay.
Whispers echo through the night,
In shadows deep, we find our light.

Each frozen breath, a secret shared,
In the stillness, hearts are bared.
Glistening shapes begin to swirl,
In this magic, time unfurl.

The crunch of snow, sweet serenade,
In the cold, a bond is made.
Figures dance with silent grace,
In this realm, we find our place.

Stars above, a scattered quilt,
Every wish, a dream fulfilled.
Underneath the icy sheen,
Shadows waltz, where hearts have been.

So let us wander, hand in hand,
Through this frost-kissed, shining land.
For in the shadows, our love ignites,
Amidst the twinkling, frozen nights.

Secrets Held Tight by Frost

In the heart of winter, secrets gleam,
Trapped beneath where silence beams.
Frozen whispers in the air,
Stories hidden everywhere.

Every crystal, a tale of old,
Years of laughter, love, and bold.
Frosted branches, a quiet trust,
Keep the secrets, as they must.

In the stillness, listen close,
Frozen hearts, where feelings dose.
Under layers, warmth resides,
In the frost, the heart confides.

Morning light breaks the silver veil,
Revealing truths in the soft exhale.
Like gentle hands, the sun will trace,
Secrets held tight, in nature's grace.

So cherish the quiet, the frost, the chill,
For within, lies a warmth to fill.
In secrets kept by winter's reign,
Love persists, through joy and pain.

The Solace of a Lonely Walk

Along the path where shadows blend,
Step by step, the heart will mend.
In solitude, a gentle song,
The echoes of where I belong.

Each footfall soft upon the earth,
A reminder of moments, of my worth.
Whispers of trees sway in the breeze,
Nature's embrace, a moment of ease.

Clouds drift lazily in the sky,
As I wander, time slips by.
With every breath, I shed the weight,
Finding solace in walking straight.

The world unfolds with each stride taken,
A journey bright, yet quietly shaken.
In lonely walks, the mind roams free,
Painting dreams of what could be.

So here I walk, where silence dwells,
In the echoes, my spirit swells.
For in the peace of a simple roam,
I find my heart, I find my home.

The Harmony of Leaf and Wind

The leaves dance lightly, with grace,
Whispers of secrets, nature's embrace.
Soft breezes carry their gentle tune,
In the sunlit glade, beneath the moon.

Branches sway, a ballet so sweet,
Amidst the green, where earth and sky meet.
Rustling melodies, a tranquil call,
The union of life, a serenade to all.

Colors burst forth, a vibrant display,
Beneath the arches, the children play.
Each rustle tells stories, of times long past,
In this harmony, the moments last.

Wind carries scents, a fragrant gift,
Through woodland paths, spirits uplift.
Nature's breath mingles, a song so clear,
In every sigh, the world draws near.

Together they weave, in a timeless dance,
In their union, we find our chance.
To breathe in deep, this world so wide,
In the harmony of leaf and wind, we abide.

Embered Remnants of Sunlight

Twilight descends, a softening glow,
The sun dips low, making shadows grow.
Embers linger, as day starts to fade,
Chasing away, the fears that we've made.

Crimson and gold paint the evening sky,
As whispers of dusk start to draw nigh.
Golden streaks kiss the horizon's line,
In the quiet stillness, the stars align.

Flickers of warmth, those fleeting feels,
Echoes of laughter, the heart it heals.
Around the corner, tomorrow will shine,
But for now, in twilight, our dreams entwine.

Each breath a moment, each sigh a prayer,
In the embers' glow, love fills the air.
Chasing the day, with its shimmering light,
We gather these remnants, into the night.

In the soft embrace of this gentle glow,
We savor the warmth that we deeply know.
As daylight whispers its sweet goodbye,
Embered remnants linger, in the vast sky.

Crystal Tears of the Sky

Morning breaks with a silvery sheen,
A tapestry woven, of bright and serene.
Dewdrops sparkle on leaves, so fair,
Like crystal tears, they hang in the air.

Each droplet holds whispers of dreams,
Captured moments, like flowing streams.
Nature's grace, in fragile attire,
Beauties collected, like notes on a lyre.

Sunrise kisses each crystal bright,
Transforming the world, with its golden light.
Glistening jewels on the green earth rest,
A glimmer of hope, in each nature's vest.

The sky weeps softly, a gentle weep,
In crystal tears, its secrets keep.
Flooded with joy, the earth drinks deep,
In silence it listens, while shadows creep.

With each tear that falls, a promise anew,
In the cycles of life, we find the true.
For in those droplets, a story flows,
Crystal tears of the sky, where beauty grows.

The Anticipation of Winter's Embrace

Frosted whispers dance on the air,
As nature prepares for the winter's care.
Leaves have fallen, a carpet of gold,
The world awaits, with a story untold.

Bare branches stretch to the cold, grey skies,
In the hush of the forest, a stillness lies.
Each breath is visible, in the crisp, fresh space,
A shiver of magic, winter's embrace.

The scent of pine lingers, sharp and sweet,
As quiet descends on the snow-padded street.
Footprints tread softly, leaving a trace,
In the world's embrace, time finds its pace.

Chill in the air, a promise so bright,
Stars twinkle softly in the deep of the night.
A blanket of white covers all in sight,
In anticipation of winter's pure light.

As days shorten and shadows arise,
The heartbeats echo beneath the skies.
With every snowfall, the earth finds grace,
In the quiet joy of winter's embrace.

Zephyrs of Change

Whispers of the evening breeze,
Carry tales of shifting seas.
In the twilight, shadows dance,
Every moment, a fleeting chance.

Golden fields sway with delight,
Promises of tomorrow's light.
Nature's canvas paints anew,
With every stroke, a vibrant hue.

Footsteps echo on the path,
Change is born from nature's wrath.
Yet in chaos, seeds are sown,
In every heart, a spark is shown.

Mountains stand, steadfast and tall,
While the rivers heed their call.
Zephyrs guide the way we roam,
Each gust a whisper, leading home.

As daybreak molds the night away,
Hope emerges in dawn's soft sway.
With every breeze, a chance to learn,
In the winds, our passions burn.

When Leaves Turn to Ghosts

In the woods where whispers dwell,
Leaves succumb, a silent spell.
Rustling hues of red and gold,
Echo tales, both young and old.

Branches bare, they reach for sky,
As daylight fades, they softly sigh.
A blanket soft, the ground adorned,
With amber dreams, the year is mourned.

Footsteps dance on crisp terrain,
Memories stitched in autumn's grain.
With every step, the echoes fade,
Ghostly forms in twilight's shade.

The sun dips low, in fiery glow,
Casting shadows, long and slow.
Leaves, like spirits, drift away,
In the chill of the closing day.

When winter calls, the ghosts take flight,
In dreams of spring, through endless night.
Yet each breath, a promise kept,
When leaves return, the world has slept.

Gossamer Threads of Cold

Threads of frost weave in the night,
Delicate whispers, shimmering light.
Silvery patterns coat the ground,
A tapestry silent, profound.

Breath of winter hangs in air,
Each exhale dances, light as care.
Gossamer strands cling to the trees,
A world transformed by winter's freeze.

Moonlight drapes a shroud so fine,
Casting shadows, a hidden line.
With every step, the silence grows,
Nature's heartbeat, a measured close.

In the stillness, time unfolds,
Stories whispered, ancient, bold.
Fragile beauty, fleeting, bright,
A moment's grace in starry night.

As dawn approaches, threads unwind,
The chill retreats, the warmth we find.
Gossamer dreams in frost remain,
In hearts where whispers still sustain.

Breath of the Frosted Dawn

Awake to shimmering skies anew,
Frosted breath, a world askew.
Nature stirs with gentle grace,
In dawn's embrace, we find our place.

Colors blend with softest hue,
A palette rich, a morning view.
With each ray, the frost does melt,
Whispers of warmth begin to felt.

Footprints mark the path we tread,
Memories linger of what has shed.
The air, crisp, with promise sings,
As daylight breaks and new life brings.

In harmony, the silence hums,
Life awakens, the heartbeat drums.
Every sunrise, a canvas fresh,
In golden light, our spirits mesh.

Breathe deep the magic of the morn,
In every chill, a promise born.
The frost once cold, now fades away,
As souls ignite in the light of day.

Beneath the Ice-Crowned Sky

Beneath the sky, so pale and bright,
The world is hushed, wrapped in white.
Silent whispers weave through frost,
In the calm, we feel the lost.

Icicles dangle from the eaves,
Glistening like crystalline leaves.
Footsteps crunch on frozen ground,
In this stillness, wisdom found.

Clouds drift slowly, shades of gray,
Marking the time of fleeting day.
Glimmers of sun, rare and fair,
Dance upon the icy air.

Frost-kissed trees reach for the sun,
In this realm, all else is done.
Nature's breath, a quiet sigh,
In harmony, we float and fly.

Beneath the stars, a twinkling sight,
The winter's quilt, pure and bright.
Wrapped in dreams, the night is near,
Beneath the ice-crowned sky, we steer.

A Journey Through the Icebound Woods

Through the woods, the frost we tread,
Each branch adorned, a silvery thread.
Nature's stillness, a gentle hand,
Guiding forth, a quiet band.

Footsteps echo in the hush,
In the snowflakes, memories rush.
Whispers of trees, ancient and old,
Secrets of winter, quietly told.

The air is sharp, a crisp embrace,
In every breath, winter's grace.
Shadows dance on the frozen stream,
Reflecting light in a glimmering dream.

Hidden paths and trails to find,
Lead us deeper, heart entwined.
Each step a story, a tale of light,
In the woods, we find our flight.

Cold winds carry a melodic tune,
Beneath the watchful, waning moon.
In the silence, our thoughts unwind,
A journey through the woods, combined.

Emerging from the icebound haze,
To greet the world, a new day's blaze.
In these woods, with spirits entwined,
We leave our doubts, the past behind.

The Twinge of Icy Breaths

Crisp morning air, it bites and nips,
As winter whispers through frozen lips.
A twinge of cold creeps through my frame,
In icy breaths, I call your name.

Each exhale hangs like a crystal sphere,
Glimmers of warmth that disappear.
Frosted cheeks and fingers numb,
Yet in this chill, my heartbeats drum.

The world around is a frozen dance,
Nature's artistry, a cold romance.
Snowflakes twirl in an endless waltz,
While echoes of laughter begin to vault.

With every breath, the air is taut,
In winter's grasp, we find what's sought.
Moments shared, beneath the freeze,
In the twinge of ice, there lies a ease.

When stars ignite the night's embrace,
We stand together, hearts in place.
Through every chill, I'll find the way,
In the twinge of icy breaths, we stay.

Shadowed Pools of Solitude

In the woods, where shadows pool,
Whispers echo, soft and cool.
The world retreats, in shades of gray,
In solitude, we find our way.

Surrounded by trees, ancient and wise,
Reflections dance in echoing sighs.
A mirror of thoughts beneath the boughs,
In this quiet realm, I make my vows.

Moonlight casts a silver hue,
On still waters, deep and true.
Each ripple speaks of dreams untold,
In shadowed pools, my heart grows bold.

The night hums sweet with nature's song,
In solitude, I feel I belong.
Bathed in silence, free from care,
In these pools of calm, I breathe the air.

Each moment lingers, rich and deep,
In the embrace of the dark, I seep.
Lost to the world and time's decree,
In shadowed pools, I find the key.

Crisp Leaves

Crisp leaves fall to the ground,
Whispers of autumn's embrace.
Golden hues all around,
Nature's soft, gentle face.

The air is fresh and clear,
Filled with scents of pine.
The season draws near,
To give way to what's divine.

Children laugh and play,
Chasing colors in the breeze.
They revel in the day,
Amongst the towering trees.

Evening shadows grow long,
As daylight starts to fade.
Nature sings her song,
In the twilight serenade.

As the sun bids adieu,
Night wraps the world in calm.
With every color anew,
Autumn holds us in her palm.

Hidden Secrets

In the forest deep and wide,
Secrets whisper through the trees.
Nature's treasures, hard to hide,
Only shared with the breeze.

Softly, shadows play and dance,
In the dappled light of day.
Every glance, a fleeting chance,
To uncover what's at bay.

Ancient stories, etched in bark,
Tell of time's elusive flight.
In the stillness, there's a spark,
Leading us to hidden light.

Nature's voice, so calm and wise,
Calls to those who seek to know.
Underneath the vast, blue skies,
A world of wonders starts to grow.

In the quiet, truth is found,
In the rustling leaves that sway.
Through the silence, profound,
The heart learns to find its way.

Echoes of Winter's Approach

Bitter winds begin to blow,
As winter edges near.
Frosty breath on tree and snow,
Whispers soft, yet clear.

The world is draped in white,
Silence blankets the land.
Stars twinkle in the night,
Guiding with a gentle hand.

Footprints crunch on icy ground,
Tales of those who have passed.
Nature's hush, a sacred sound,
In the stillness, ice holds fast.

Firelight flickers and glows,
Chasing shadows far away.
In the night, warmth grows,
As the cold begins to sway.

Each flake tells a story old,
Of where it's been and seen.
As winter nights unfold,
Hope blooms soft and serene.

Misty Mornings and Quiet Hues

Misty mornings greet the day,
Softening the world we see.
In this peaceful, gentle way,
Nature wraps us quietly.

Blankets of fog hover low,
Embracing fields and streams.
In silence, wonders flow,
Weaving through our dreams.

Colors muted, soft and shy,
The sun tries to break through.
A palette painted in the sky,
Drenched with every hue.

Birds begin to chirp and sing,
In harmony with the dawn.
Awakening, life takes wing,
As the mist starts to yawn.

Each breath a moment cherished,
In the stillness, we find grace.
With every trace, fears are perished,
In this tranquil, wondrous space.

The Last Dance of Golden Days

As day fades to a gentle close,
The sun dips low in the sky.
Golden hues in warm, soft glows,
Bid farewell with a sigh.

Leaves rustle in the evening breeze,
Nature's song begins to play.
A symphony among the trees,
Celebrating the day's stay.

Stars twinkle, shy at first light,
As twilight wraps the streets.
The world shines with pure delight,
Where day and night softly meet.

As shadows stretch and weave,
The air whispers with past grace.
In every heart, we believe,
In the warmth of time and space.

Golden days now take their bow,
In the dance of setting sun.
A gentle hush, and here and now,
Life's last notes have just begun.

Dance of the Winter Spirits

In the chill of night they swirl,
Shadows weave and softly twirl,
Frosty whispers fill the air,
Nature's secrets laid aware.

Glittering on the frozen ground,
Echoes of their presence found,
With each step, a memory,
A tale lost in reverie.

They glide through trees with gentle grace,
Stars reflected in their face,
Winter's breath a soft caress,
In this dance, we find our rest.

Silent nights hold them near,
Every heartbeat, crystal clear,
In moonlit dreams, they start to play,
Guiding souls who've lost their way.

When the dawn begins to break,
Leave behind what we can't take,
Yet in our hearts, they will stay,
With the light of every day.

The Edge of Tomorrow's Warmth

Whispers of dawn begin to rise,
Painting gold in the skies,
Promises held in morning light,
Hope reflects a future bright.

With every step on dew-kissed grass,
We gather strength as moments pass,
Clutching dreams, both near and far,
Guided softly by our star.

Hearts ablaze with fierce desire,
Fueling the eternal fire,
At the edge of what could be,
We find power to break free.

Across the horizon's gentle bend,
New beginnings there to send,
A journey forged through light and dark,
In every soul, a vital spark.

As the sun welcomes the day,
Shadows fade, they slip away,
A bright promise found in sight,
At the edge, everything feels right.

A Breath of Silent Acceptance

In the calm where shadows meet,
Whispers sound like soft retreat,
Finding peace in silent sighs,
As the past no longer cries.

Moments linger on the breeze,
Carried through the rustling leaves,
Letting go of heavy weight,
Accepting all that comes with fate.

The heart learns to mend its pain,
In the dance of sun and rain,
Every tear a story told,
A blessing wrapped in threads of gold.

Quiet strength now fills the air,
Every heartbeat stripped so bare,
Here, in stillness, we embrace,
Life's gentle flow, a warm embrace.

A breath drawn deep, released with grace,
Moving forward to find our place,
In acceptance, we are whole,
A journey that deepens the soul.

In the Heart of a Snowbound Dream

Drifting softly, a wisp of white,
Blankets cover the earth at night,
In dreams we wander, lost yet found,
In winter's hush, a sacred sound.

Every flake a whispered thought,
Casting spells that time forgot,
Through the silence, stories bloom,
In the stillness, thoughts consume.

A world transformed in silver light,
Where even shadows dance in flight,
Hearts entwined in frosty air,
In every breath, hope meets despair.

The stars above, they gleam and sway,
Guiding paths through night and day,
Seeking solace, warm and deep,
In the dreams that winter keeps.

Awake, we carry what we find,
Fragments bright in hearts and mind,
In the winter's soft embrace,
The dreams remain, a sacred place.

Frosted Dreams on Silent Nights

Whispers dance in frozen air,
Stars above, a silver flare.
Shadows wrap the world in white,
Frosted dreams on silent nights.

Moonlight paints a gentle glow,
Crisp and cool, the soft winds blow.
Crystals form on frosted ground,
In this peace, pure magic found.

Thoughts arise like mist at dawn,
Silent secrets softly drawn.
Gentle sighs of winter's breath,
Embrace the stillness, dance with death.

In the hush, time stands so still,
Nature's song, a tranquil thrill.
Memories wrapped in softest chill,
Frosted dreams our hearts distill.

Through the night, the echoes play,
Tender thoughts that softly sway.
In the quiet, souls unite,
Frosted dreams on silent nights.

The Call of the Frosted Earth

Whispers ride on icy winds,
Nature's voice, where silence begins.
Frosted fields, a crisp embrace,
In their stillness, time finds grace.

Underneath a sky so dark,
Crickets hush, and night's a spark.
Footprints traced in glistening dew,
Following paths that feel so new.

Each breath clouds in chilly air,
Awakening the heart to care.
The earth calls with a soft, sweet song,
Winter's cloak, where we belong.

Stars above, a guiding light,
Leading dreams through velvet night.
Frosted whispers, gentle cheer,
Embrace the calm, hold it near.

In the night, the magic swells,
Frosted earth, where wonder dwells.
Every glimmer, every spark,
Guides us closer through the dark.

Twilight's Breath of Silence

Daning shadows, hues collide,
In twilight's grasp, we softly bide.
Whispers swirl as day departs,
Silence reigns in quiet hearts.

Colors fade, the horizon sighs,
Stars awaken in velvet skies.
Along the path where visions play,
Twilight beckons, showing the way.

Glimmers of light, a gentle trace,
Lead us to that sacred space.
In the hush, the night unfolds,
Twilight's breath of silence holds.

Time drifts softly, moments blend,
Every heartbeat a soothing friend.
Linger here, where dreams ignite,
In twilight's calm, all feels right.

As silence cloaks the world around,
Magic whispers, dreams abound.
Hold this peace, forever stay,
Twilight's breath, our guide today.

The Vanishing Warmth

When daylight yields to colder nights,
The vanishing warmth, a soft plight.
Embers fade in the hearth's embrace,
Chilled air whispers of time and space.

Once bright flames now dim and gray,
Fleeting moments drift away.
Tender voices start to fade,
In the hush, sweet warmth betrayed.

Golden memories ebb and flow,
As shadows stretch and soft winds blow.
Each heartbeat a reminder stark,
Of warmth that once lit up the dark.

A fading glow, a lingering ache,
Beneath the frost, our hearts awake.
Touched by time, yet still we yearn,
For every flame, a chance to burn.

The chill may bite, yet love will stay,
To guard the warmth that fades away.
In every heart, the fire will gleam,
The vanishing warmth, a tender dream.

The Glistening Veil

In the dawn's soft light, it glimmers bright,
A tapestry woven with threads of white.
Nature's embrace, a delicate show,
Whispers of magic in the world below.

Beneath the trees, the shadows play,
Casting dreams that drift away.
A veil so fine, it cloaks the morn,
As day awakens, the night is shorn.

Each droplet hangs like a precious gem,
Reflecting colors in the diadem.
A silent dance on every branch,
Where beauty reigns, and hearts shall quench.

Through frosty breath, the air is still,
Mingling with hopes, a winter thrill.
In every nook, the silence sleeps,
Secrets wrapped in the snow that keeps.

As twilight falls, the sparkle fades,
Yet in the heart, the memory stays.
A glistening veil, a fleeting whim,
In the soul's soft sigh, lies the hymn.

Snowflakes in the Twilight

As daylight fades, the chill descends,
Snowflakes dance, the evening bends.
Each flake unique, a fleeting gem,
Whispering tales as they fall, condemn.

Twilight wraps the world in gray,
Softly, gently, it holds the day.
The hush of night, a soothing balm,
While snowflakes swirl in a winter charm.

Glistening softly on barren trees,
Adorned with crystals, a gentle tease.
The sky reveals its shimm'ring art,
As snowflakes drift, they touch the heart.

In this quiet, where dreams ignite,
The world adorned in purest white.
Each frozen crystal, a moment to keep,
A memory painted, a promise deep.

The stars awaken, the moonlight glows,
The night unfolds, and wonder flows.
Snowflakes whisper in the still,
As dreams entwine with the night's soft chill.

Frozen Echoes of Yesterday

Beneath the snow, where stories sleep,
Frozen echoes, secrets to keep.
Faint memories rise from the icy ground,
Whispers of joy in silence found.

The shadows dance in the pale moonlight,
Casting memories of a long-lost flight.
Each flake that falls, a tale to spin,
Of laughter, of warmth, where love had been.

Time holds its breath, in crystal clear,
Sculpting moments we once held dear.
Through frigid air, the past draws near,
In every heartbeat, we still can hear.

The winds of change, they softly sigh,
Tales of yesterday that linger nigh.
In the frost, a memory glows,
A bridge to what the heart still knows.

Underneath the blanket, stories unfold,
Treasured remembrances, shiny and bold.
Frozen echoes, forever they stay,
In the heart's chamber, they light the way.

The Coming of Stillness

In the twilight hours, stillness arrives,
A blanket of peace, where nature thrives.
Softly it whispers through branches bare,
Inviting the world to breathe in the air.

The brook's soft murmur drowns in the night,
As shadows embrace the fading light.
Each star appears in the deepening hue,
A promise of solace, calmness anew.

The chill in the air holds stories away,
Echoes of life in the quiet ballet.
Each gust of wind carries a sigh,
Wrapped in the stillness, as hours go by.

With every heartbeat, the world finds rest,
Nestled in memories, a gentle quest.
The silence deepens, like a lullaby,
Cradling dreams as they whisper and fly.

As night stretches forth, the shadows blend,
Time seems to linger, refusing to end.
In this moment where stillness reigns,
We find our peace, as the heart contains.

A Shiver Runs Through the Grove

In the hush of twilight, stillness reigns,
Whispers of leaves stir the autumn plains.
A cold breeze weaves through the branch's arms,
Cradling the night with its fleeting charms.

Moonlight spills through boughs, silver and bright,
Casting soft shadows that dance in the night.
Each crackle of frost, a secret untold,
A shiver runs through the grove, brave and bold.

The air holds a magic, crisp and divine,
Nature's own whispers entwined in the pine.
A blanket of stars cloaks the whispered air,
Holds the promise of dreams that drift everywhere.

In this tranquil haven, time seems to cease,
The heart finds a rhythm, a pulse of peace.
With every soft sound, the world fades away,
In the grove's gentle heart, night turns to day.

So linger a while where the shadows play,
And let the cool embrace of the twilight sway.
For in the stillness, there's beauty to find,
A shiver runs through the grove, heart intertwined.

Twilight's Frosted Promise

The day bows low as the sun takes flight,
Casting long shadows, embracing the night.
A shimmer of frost crowns each silent hill,
Twilight's promise whispers, soft and still.

Stars peek shyly from their velvet drapes,
While the world wraps itself in frosty shapes.
In the coolness lingers a delicate glow,
Nature's sweet sigh as the night starts to flow.

The whispering winds carry secrets untold,
Each breath of the night, a story unfolds.
The air, laced with sweetness, invites us to stay,
In twilight's embrace, let the moment play.

Frost-kissed petals wilt, yet still they shine,
Embodied hope in a fragile line.
Through the quiet glen where dreams start to roam,
Twilight's frosted promise brings us back home.

As darkness deepens, the colors will blend,
In the heart of the night, our spirits ascend.
With every soft gust, the stars start to gleam,
Twilight's frosted promise weaves into a dream.

Nature's Breath of Icy Kisses

A canvas of white drapes the world in peace,
Nature exhales softly, a moment's release.
The air is laced with crystalline delight,
An icy caress awakens the night.

Trees wear their crowns of shimmering glass,
Glimmers of silver where tender paths pass.
Each rustle and crunch speaks the language of cold,
Nature's breath of kisses, gentle and bold.

Underneath the heavens, the stars brightly sing,
Beneath the chill, there's a warmth in the spring.
A promise that lingers in every flake's fall,
Nature bids us listen, it beckons us all.

In this frosted embrace, the world finds its grace,
As the dance of the snowflakes unveils their trace.
With hearts wide open, we welcome the night,
Embracing the magic of winter's soft light.

So step into the silence, where dreams intertwine,
Let nature's breath guide you, your spirit align.
For in every icy kiss, there's a wish to restore,
Nature's breath of icy kisses, forevermore.

Glistening Paths under Dimming Skies

As the day draws to close, colors start to fade,
Glistening paths emerge, in twilight arrayed.
Each step on the gravel sparkles like stars,
Whispers of wonder beneath Venus and Mars.

The trees arch their backs, cradling the light,
Their leaves soft and gold against the darkening sight.
A trail of soft glimmers leads hearts to explore,
Under the canopy, the world asks for more.

Stars begin twinkling, igniting the shroud,
Cerulean dreams drift on vaporous cloud.
Nature unfolds like a carefully sewn quilt,
In the heart of the night, all worries are spilt.

Footprints may follow where spirits have roamed,
Finding solace in magic, together they foamed.
In this luminous dance, where shadows collide,
The glistening paths shine, with wonders inside.

So walk with the night, let your soul dive deep,
In glistening paths, find your heart's tender keep.
For under dimming skies, magic resides,
In every sweet moment, where beauty abides.

Ethereal Touch of the Frost

A whisper softly graces night,
As stars adorn the velvet sky.
The world, it shimmers, pure and bright,
In winter's breath, we softly lie.

Each blade of grass a diamond crowned,
Embraced by chilly, tender air.
The silence sings, no rushing sound,
In stillness, peace is found, so rare.

A dance of shadows on the ground,
With frost like lace on boughs and stone.
The sun reveals, with warmth profound,
That magic waits, though we're alone.

In every flake, a tale unfolds,
Of nature's art, both bold and sweet.
In fleeting moments, life beholds,
The beauty found beneath our feet.

So wander 'neath this silver sheen,
And listen to the night's soft breath.
For in this world, so lush, so green,
We find the grace of life and death.

Beneath the Silver Lace

Moonlight weaves a silken thread,
Across the fields where shadows play.
The world beneath its soft caress,
Awakens dreams that drift away.

A quilt of white, where whispers glide,
Inscribed with secrets, old and new.
Each step a memory that hides,
Beneath the silver, soft and true.

The trees like sentinels stand tall,
With limbs adorned in glistening frost.
In winter's grasp, the echoes call,
Of moments gained and moments lost.

The air is crisp, the night is calm,
A lullaby of stars above.
In every breath, a soothing balm,
A gentle touch from those we love.

So let the silver lace enchant,
And guide your heart through twilight's maze.
For life is but a fleeting chant,
Beneath the glow of moonlit days.

Ripples of a Forgotten Chill

Upon the lake, the ice resounds,
Its surface mirrors winter's breath.
With every crack, a story found,
Of nature's silence, love, and death.

The trees weep softly, branches bowed,
Their leaves have whispered tales of yore.
In haunting beauty, they're enshrouded,
Echoes of laughter on the shore.

Each ripple spreads like fading light,
Yet holds the warmth of days long past.
A fleeting glimpse into the night,
Where shadows dance, and dreams are cast.

For in the chill, a heart might mend,
And find the peace that still resides.
In frozen depths, the spirits blend,
With memories that never hide.

So pause a while, remember well,
The ripples left upon the stream.
In every heart, a hidden bell,
Awaits to ring a silent dream.

The Weight of the Fallen Snow

The world is hushed, a canvas white,
A blanket soft that hugs the ground.
Each flake a star, a touch of light,
In winter's hold, our hearts are found.

The branches bow beneath the load,
A testament to nature's art.
In silence, pathways gently goad,
Us to embrace a quiet heart.

The chill reminds us to take pause,
In moments wrapped in crystal lace.
The weight of snow brings subtle cause,
For reflection in this frozen space.

With every step, a muffled sound,
As if the earth is holding breath.
In snowy realms, we're tightly bound,
To life and dreams, in whispers left.

So let the snowfall guide your way,
Through winter's grasp, where dreams still flow.
In every flake, a bright ballet,
We find the weight of love's own glow.

Frosted Footprints on the Ground

In the quiet dawn's embrace,
Frosted prints in white lace.
Soft whispers of winter's breath,
Trace a story of life and death.

Rising sun, the chill will fade,
Yet the memories won't evade.
Each step tells of paths once trod,
Nature's canvas, painted broad.

Beneath the trees, the silence glows,
As the shimmering cold wind blows.
Footprints lead to dreams unseen,
In a world painted fresh and clean.

Morning dew on the grass does gleam,
In the sparkling light, we dream.
Frosted trails towards the sky,
Where the whispers of wonder lie.

With every step, a tale unfolds,
In the warmth the sunrise holds.
Frosted footprints, where we roam,
Mapping out a journey home.

A Tapestry of Silver and Gold

In the twilight's gentle weave,
Threads of silver, dreams believe.
Golden hues in evening's glow,
Woven tales from long ago.

Stars above begin to dance,
Filling hearts with hope's romance.
Each twinkle, a whispered tale,
In this fabric, love won't fail.

Curtains drawn on daylight's play,
Night unfolds in rich array.
A tapestry of time and light,
Thread by thread, we stitch the night.

Every moment, a stitch anew,
Crafting paths that we pursue.
Look closely, and you will find,
Stories woven, intertwined.

In the fabric of our dreams,
Life reflects in silver beams.
Together in this sacred art,
A tapestry of soul and heart.

Shadows Lengthen in the Stillness

As the sun dips low and fades,
Longing quiet, our serenade.
Shadows stretch across the ground,
In the stillness, peace is found.

Gentle whispers fill the air,
Inviting souls to linger there.
Softly, night begins to creep,
Cradling dreams as we retreat.

Trees cast silhouettes so tall,
Embracing night with silent call.
Echoes of the day now sleep,
In the darkness, secrets keep.

Every shadow tells a tale,
Of joy and sorrow, love's unveiled.
In still moments, hearts align,
As we dance with the divine.

Stars awaken, twinkling bright,
Guardians of the velvet night.
In the stillness, shadows blend,
A quiet promise without end.

Wistful Whispers of the Night Breeze

In the hush of evening's near,
Wistful whispers, soft and clear.
Night breeze carries tales untold,
Gentle sighs, like dreams of old.

Moonlight bathes the world in grace,
As shadows play in twilight space.
Every breath a lullaby,
Inviting hearts to gently fly.

Rustling leaves, a sweet embrace,
Nature's rhythm, time and place.
Winds of change caress the skin,
A dance of dusk where dreams begin.

Echoes call from distant shores,
Wistful thoughts, the heart adores.
In the softest night's decree,
We find solace, wild and free.

Let the night weave magic wide,
In whispered tones, we shall confide.
Through the dreams of night we tread,
On wistful whispers, love is spread.

Sullen Clouds Over Serene Hills

Sullen clouds drift across the sky,
Whispers of gray in a silent cry.
Hills stand solemn, cloaked in shade,
Nature's beauty, now delayed.

Beneath the weight of gloomy veils,
Life's vibrant song slowly pales.
Yet a flicker, a glint of light,
Holds hope's promise in the night.

A soft breeze stirs the heavy air,
Carrying secrets, weight, and care.
Serenity finds a quiet pause,
As hearts yearn for nature's cause.

Mountains sigh under the clouded dome,
Searching for a sunlit home.
In the silence, dreams take flight,
Longing for the kiss of light.

Though shadows linger, time will heal,
A tender warmth, soft and real.
Sullen clouds, they will disperse,
Unfolding life in universe.

Ethereal Glimmers of the Foxfire

Ethereal glimmers dance in the night,
Foxfire flickers, a magical light.
Soft whispers echo through the trees,
Nature's secrets carried by the breeze.

Beneath the cloak of the midnight shade,
Mysteries of twilight gently played.
Each glow a tale, timeless and bright,
Woven in shadows, woven in light.

The forest breathes with a living pulse,
As stars awaken and shadows convulse.
Fleeting moments, they'll soon take flight,
Captured in dreams, lost to the night.

A shimmer of hope in the dense black air,
An invitation, a sweetened dare.
Explore the paths where wonders hide,
Embrace the magic, let joy glide.

As dawn approaches, these dreams will fade,
But echoes of night will never trade.
Ethereal glimmers shall always stay,
In hearts and minds, forever play.

The Grapes of Gloom

The grapes hang heavy on the vine,
Wrapped in shadows, dark and fine.
Harvest whispers, tinged with sorrow,
Promises lost to a bleak tomorrow.

Violet skins, like cloaks of night,
Hiding stories, hidden from sight.
In the vineyard's grasp, time stands still,
Fading dreams beneath the hill.

Each droplet of dew tells a tale,
Of laughter and joy, now frail.
Sour the taste, bittersweet the chime,
Echoes of laughter lost to time.

Yet as the seasons turn from fine,
New blooms will sprout on the vine.
Grapes of gloom may darkly cling,
But hope shall rise on the wings of spring.

In the heart, a spark takes hold,
Tales of resilience quietly unfold.
Though the grapes bear a mournful tune,
Life will blossom beneath the moon.

Nightfall's Icy Breath

Nightfall's icy breath draws near,
Chilling shadows, instilling fear.
Stars appear like distant dreams,
As silence swallows daytime screams.

Beneath the frost, the world lies still,
Time suspended on a frozen hill.
The moon casts silver, sharp and bright,
Transforming darkness into light.

Whispers of winter caress the ground,
Nature's lullaby, a haunting sound.
As branches dance in a frosty sway,
The heart finds warmth in the cold's display.

A frozen lake mirrors the sky,
While shadows linger, spirits cry.
Yet within this chill, a fire glows,
In hidden corners where warm winds blow.

Nightfall's icy breath may weave despair,
But beneath the frost, life is fair.
As dawn breaks free from winter's shroud,
Hope awakens, fierce and proud.

Shadows in the Hazy Light

In twilight's embrace, shadows softly creep,
Whispers of dreams in silence seep.
Figures dance where the light fades low,
Caught in a moment, time moves slow.

The world is painted in shades of gray,
As dusk settles in, night takes the day.
Glimmers of hope flicker in the dark,
Lost in the echoes, we search for the spark.

A breeze carries secrets, old as the trees,
Fate intertwines like branches in a breeze.
As horizons blend, realities blur,
In shadows of twilight, hearts start to stir.

Yet in this stillness, a pulse remains,
Love's gentle touch, through joy and pains.
Together we wander, guided by light,
In the hazy allure of a softening night.

Though shadows may linger, we dare to fight,
Breaching the dark with courage and might.
For even in shadows, hope finds a way,
A promise of dawn at the break of day.

An Invitation from the North

Whispers of winter carried on the breeze,
The North beckons softly, inviting us, please.
Crisp air calls to wanderers far and wide,
To chase the horizon where the wild spirits ride.

Snowflakes dance gently, a delicate swirl,
Nature's pure magic, a beautiful pearl.
Mountains stand tall, draped in white,
A promise of wonder in the still of the night.

Crackling fires await with warmth in their glow,
Sharing tales of the frost and the snow.
Laughter resounds in the cold, crisp air,
An invitation to linger and share.

As starlit skies blanket the sleeping ground,
The Northern lights weave stories around.
Dreams intertwine with the breath of the cold,
An invitation from the North, pure and bold.

In every snow-covered branch and leaf,
Nature whispers softly, a beautiful brief.
An adventure awaits, let your heart soar,
An invitation from the North, forevermore.

Frost-Kissed Memories

In the silence of winter, memories glisten bright,
Frost-kissed moments bathed in soft light.
Every breath a whisper, held in the air,
A tapestry woven with tender care.

Laughter echoes from days long past,
Each snowflake a memory, too precious to last.
Footprints in powder lead the way home,
Through fields of white, we love and we roam.

Twilight unfolds with a magical glow,
As stars awaken in the blanket of snow.
Hearts wrapped in warmth, we gather around,
The stories of frost in the stillness abound.

Embers flicker, warming the night,
Embracing the frost with a comforting light.
Nostalgia dances in the icy air,
Frost-kissed memories, beyond compare.

Through whispers of winter, we find our way,
In the cold embrace, the heart comes to play.
Frost-kissed reflections that time cannot sever,
In memories we hold, we live on forever.

Threads of Icy Silence

In the depth of the night, a silence prevails,
Threads of ice weaving delicate trails.
Nature holds breath, as if time stands still,
Wrapped in the quiet, the world feels the chill.

Frost clings to branches, a shimmering lace,
In the heart of the winter, we find our place.
Every crystal a story, ancient yet new,
In the tapestry woven of cold and of blue.

Voices are hushed, as the stars twinkle bright,
Under the blanket of soft, velvety night.
The moon holds vigil, casting shadows long,
Embracing the stillness, a serene, gentle song.

Among the echoes, the heart speaks loud,
Finding connections hidden in the shroud.
Through threads of icy silence, warmth comes alive,
In the depths of the winter, our spirits survive.

So let us linger where the frozen trees stand,
Embracing the beauty scattered by hand.
In the land of quiet whispers, we hear love call,
In threads of icy silence, we find strength in it all.

Whispers of Autumn's Breath

Leaves dance softly to the ground,
As breezes hum a gentle tune.
Crisp air carries memories around,
While sunsets blush beneath the moon.

Fires crackle in warm embrace,
Pumpkin spice fills up the air.
Nature dons a golden lace,
Inviting all to linger there.

Birds prepare to take their flight,
While clouds drift lazily along.
Days grow short, yet hearts feel light,
In autumn's grip, we all belong.

The trees wear crowns of amber gold,
As whispers weave through bough and branch.
Stories of the year unfold,
In tender moments, dreams can prance.

Together we shall walk this path,
Through rustling leaves and fading light.
With every step, we share a laugh,
As autumn's breath ignites the night.

Frosted Veils of Dawn

Morning breaks in shades of grey,
A misty veil cloaks the land.
Frosty breath of winter's sway,
Kissing earth with gentle hand.

The world transforms, a glimmer bright,
Each blade of grass a diamond's gleam.
Soft whispers echo, pure delight,
As nature wakes from slumber's dream.

A hush envelops all that's near,
While shadows stretch in timid form.
With every breath, the chill draws near,
Embracing all in winter's charm.

Trees stand tall, in white adorned,
Their branches cradle winter's thread.
With every step, new tales are born,
In frosted fields where dreams are fed.

As sunlight breaks, the day will bloom,
A tapestry of warmth and grace.
The frost will fade, yet still loom,
In memory's heart, a soft embrace.

The Tingle of October's Caress

October whispers in the breeze,
With colors bold and laughter bright.
Crisp air dances through the trees,
As days fade softly into night.

The harvest moon begins to rise,
A lantern hung in velvet skies.
Night's embrace brings sweet surprise,
As stars blink down, like little eyes.

Pumpkins smile on porches wide,
With candlelight and stories spun.
In haunted woods, we walk with pride,
In shadows cast by setting sun.

A tingle runs through heart and hand,
As whispers haunt the silent air.
We gather close to understand,
The magic found in autumn's care.

Each moment cherished, sweet and clear,
With laughter shared and friendship's call.
In October's grip, we find our cheer,
Embraced within love's gentle thrall.

Shadows in the Fading Light

Shadows stretch across the land,
As daylight bids the world goodbye.
The sun descends with golden hand,
Painting the dusk in hues that sigh.

Evening whispers on the breeze,
Carrying tales of day gone by.
Stars appear with gentle ease,
Winking softly from the sky.

Footsteps echo down the lane,
Shrouded in the twilight's grasp.
Memories linger, sweet yet plain,
In the twilight's quiet clasp.

The night unfolds its velvet cloak,
Embracing all in tender care.
With every heartbeat, dreams invoke,
A magic found in moonlit air.

As shadows dance and silence sings,
We find our peace in nature's light.
In moments shared, our heartstrings cling,
To whispers soft, in fading light.

Crisp Secrets of the Twilight Hour

The sun fades low behind the trees,
Shadows stretch and dance with ease.
A breeze carries whispers soft and light,
Secrets hidden in the coming night.

Stars begin to twinkle, one by one,
The fading day now nearly done.
In dusk's embrace, all feels so near,
A perfect moment, crystal clear.

The air turns cool, yet hearts are warm,
Nature's rhythm, a soothing balm.
Time slows down, a cherished glance,
In twilight's hush, we find our chance.

The world transforms in gentle hues,
Each shadow tells a tale to muse.
Underneath this vast expanse,
We find our peace, we find our stance.

Embrace the secrets softly spun,
Beneath the gaze of the setting sun.
In quiet moments, we take a bow,
To life's crisp secrets of the hour.

Gales of a Distant Season

Whispers through the autumn leaves,
Gales that tug at time and eves.
Crisp and clear, a change is near,
Echoes of a season we hold dear.

The branches sway in a lively dance,
Colors swirl in a wild romance.
Golden browns and fiery reds,
Nature's palette before winter spreads.

With every gust, a story told,
Of ancient woods and hearts so bold.
The chilling air, sweet with pine,
As daylight fades, the stars align.

A moment caught, a fleeting sight,
In the swirling gales of night.
The distant whispers call us near,
Reminding us what we hold dear.

While seasons change, we still remain,
In every storm, in every strain.
With hearts united, we brave the skies,
In gales that tease, in whispered sighs.

Where Warmth Meets Winter's Edge

A blanket of frost on the windowpane,
Soft whispers of snow begin to wane.
Fireplace crackles, a dance of desire,
Inviting us close to its welcoming fire.

Outside, the world wears a glistening coat,
While inside, hearts warm like a gentle note.
Sipping cocoa, wrapped in delight,
In the cozy embrace of a softly lit night.

Footprints of winter trace through the ground,
Each step taken, a magical sound.
Where warmth meets the chill, and love begins,
In every moment, a story spins.

The laughter echoes, bright and clear,
In this season when joy draws near.
Holding hands, we cherish the time,
Where warmth meets winter in a perfect rhyme.

As days grow short and nights extend,
In every flicker, in every friend.
We find our comfort, we find our pledge,
Where warmth beautifully meets winter's edge.

Whispered Tales Beneath the Stars

Beneath the sky, a canvas spread,
Constellations weave the tales we've read.
Each star a spark, a memory shared,
Whispered secrets of love declared.

Sitting close, we gaze in awe,
Nature's magic, its silent law.
Stories held in the moon's embrace,
Soft light dancing on every face.

The night air hums with ancient lore,
Echoes of dreams from days of yore.
In every heartbeat, a tale unfolds,
Of hopes and wishes, of hearts so bold.

As shadows deepen, we breathe in tight,
The wonders waiting in the night.
With every twinkle, new adventures call,
In whispered tales, we surrender all.

Together we weave, with laughter and tears,
In this shared moment, we conquer fears.
Beneath the stars, where dreams roam free,
Whispered tales unfold for you and me.

Echoes Beneath the Frosty Boughs

Whispers weave through icy trees,
Echoes dance on winter's breeze.
Footprints fade in glistening snow,
Silent tales from long ago.

Branches bow with crystal weight,
Nature's pause, a solemn state.
Frozen laughter on the air,
Hushed reflections everywhere.

Evening falls with muted light,
Stars awaken, pierce the night.
Crimson skies turn soft and grey,
As shadows quietly play.

Underneath the frosty leaves,
Nature breathes, and softly grieves.
Heartbeats sync with winter's song,
In this hush, we all belong.

Waiting for the thaw to come,
Life returns with beating drum.
But for now, in stillness stand,
Echoes held in nature's hand.

A Tinge of Restlessness

Beneath the calm, a current flows,
Restless thoughts where no one goes.
Whispers call from distant lands,
Yearning hearts, like grains of sand.

Clouds swirl brightly in the sky,
As dreams take wing, and spirits fly.
Nighttime secrets, hushed and deep,
Awake the soul from peaceful sleep.

Lonely winds begin to sigh,
Echoing a soft goodbye.
Moonlit shadows flicker past,
Moments fleeting, never last.

Outside, the world grows still tonight,
While dreams draw close and shadows light.
In every echo, a glint of chance,
A tinge of hope calls us to dance.

With every breath, the longing stirs,
In the heart where freedom purrs.
We chase the dawn, the endless quest,
For in this moment, we find rest.

Fragments of Winter's Breath

Delicate flakes on the windowpane,
Each one a story, none the same.
Whispers of cold greet the dawn,
As night drapes softly, then is gone.

Frosty patterns lace the trees,
Nature's art in the freezing breeze.
Each breath fogs the air around,
In silence, beauty can be found.

The world adorned in white and grey,
Hushed and waiting for the day.
Echoes of laughter filled the air,
Now the stillness reigns everywhere.

Time stands still in the icy world,
Gentle dreams are softly unfurled.
A dance of seasons, pure and bright,
Fragments caught in soft winter's light.

Moments linger, frozen in time,
As nature whispers its quiet rhyme.
With each heartbeat, we feel the pulse,
Of winter's breath, a tender impulse.

Ghostly Breezes Through Empty Streets

Moonlight drapes the silent town,
Ghostly breezes, whispers drown.
Echoes haunt the cobblestone,
In the stillness, dreams are sown.

Windows darken, shadows creep,
The world has drifted into sleep.
Yet beneath the calm façade,
Lingering memories make us nod.

Footsteps fade on winding lanes,
Carried softly like gentle rains.
Faded laughter from days of yore,
In the stillness, we recall more.

Every alley, every lane,
Holds a story, love, and pain.
As the night wraps secrets tight,
Ghostly breezes stir the night.

And in this chill, we find our way,
Through silent moments, gone astray.
For in the dark, we sense a spark,
Of life that hums beneath the dark.

A Symphony of Frost

In the stillness of the night,
Whispers dance on silver air.
Crystals form a quiet light,
Nature's beauty laid so bare.

Each breath hangs in frigid grace,
Breathless marvel, crystal game.
Footprints trace a fleeting space,
As the world forgets its name.

Branches bow with weight of dreams,
A symphony, soft and low.
Frosty threads in moonlit beams,
Weaving stories, calm and slow.

Frosty fingers touch the ground,
Painting landscapes cold yet bright.
Nature's canvas, beauty found,
In the depths of winter's night.

Harmony in every chill,
Echoes linger in the breeze.
A quiet magic, cold and still,
In the heart of frozen trees.

Of Longing and Icy Caresses

In the absence of the sun,
Whispers weave through icy nights.
Lonesome hearts that never run,
Yearning for the warmth of lights.

Shadows stretch in silver gleam,
Caresses made of frost and air.
Dreams interlace in a dream,
As the winter's chill lays bare.

The world below, a quiet sigh,
Fingers brush against the cold.
A gentle call, a soft goodbye,
In the stories left untold.

Longing stirs with frozen breath,
In the stillness, time stands still.
Every moment hints at death,
And yet sparks a hopeful thrill.

Through the mist, a glimmer glows,
Hearts entwined in cold's embrace.
Icy paths where longing flows,
Finding warmth in frozen space.

Beyond the Edge of Warmth

Snowflakes drift from skies of grey,
Whispers soft of winter's tune.
Beyond the edge where shadows play,
Glows a memory of June.

Frosted dreams on brittle leaves,
A promise held in frozen air.
Each breath lingers, yet deceives,
As warm dreams rise beyond despair.

Frozen rivers map a path,
Stories etched in white and blue.
In the silence, echoes wrath,
Yet, beneath, the warmth is true.

Footprints mark the journey's end,
While the cold wraps tight like night.
Beyond the edge, where heart can mend,
The spark of warmth ignites the light.

In this realm, both dark and bright,
Life resides in winter's clutch.
Finding solace, holding tight,
To the warmth we crave so much.

Shattered Sunlight on Frozen Paths

Golden rays break through the chill,
Dance like diamonds on the ice.
Reality bends to will,
In this realm of cold and spice.

Each step crackles, shards of light,
Scattered fragments on the ground.
Winter's beauty takes its flight,
In the silence, joy is found.

Colors shimmer, warm and bright,
Draped across a landscape white.
Shattered sunbeams, pure delight,
Catching dreams in purest light.

Frozen paths of glimmering lore,
Where the sun and shadows play.
Echoes whisper, hearts explore,
Every moment, fleeting day.

In this dance of cold and sun,
Nature's art unveils our fate.
Harmonies of light begun,
On frozen paths, we resonate.

Milton Keynes UK
Ingram Content Group UK Ltd.
UKHW010228111224
452348UK00011B/594